Belonging

Also by Martin Anderson

MARTIN ANDERSON

Belonging

followed by

The *English* Boat

Shearsman Books
Exeter

First published in the United Kingdom in 2009 by
Shearsman Books Ltd
58 Velwell Road
Exeter EX4 4LD

ISBN 978-1-84861-037-8

Acknowledgements
Grateful acknowledgement is made to the editors of the following
magazines in which some of these poems, sometimes in a different form
and under a different title, first appeared: *Fire; High Chair; Oasis; Other
Poetry; Poetry Salzburg; Shearsman; The Journal; Tremblestone.*

'Occulta', 'A Boyhood' and 'Light Where There Is' (originally titled 'The
Resources') appeared as a broadsheet published by Oasis Books, London,
in 2002.

CONTENTS

A World Impatient to Sound

A Constructed Place

Residues of Light and Air

The *English* Boat

The man who finds his country sweet is only a raw beginner; the man for whom each country is as his own is already strong; but only the man for whom the whole world is as a foreign country is perfect.

—Hugh St Victor

A World Impatient to Sound

Occulta

That it is
not
worth waiting
for, that
the eye blinks
in a damp
cellarage, watching

doors slam
on it, and all
the room's shadows

face glimpsed
in a window,
a life
looking out
on a life,
crossing streets
entering a house

smell of warm dinners
under corrugated iron roof,
plash of fen
round lacerated knees,
cress pulled
from clear waters

where light
crossed, over the hand
and found
a voice, a consolation
thumb
print upon
fogged mirrors
shadow, breaking
upon others,
in church porches,
under rose-lapped gables,

to echo,
and to order
opaque realities
— yours —
mingled,
mint and creosote,
till one thing became
another

without really meaning to,
in a dispersion
of phonemes

the gold effluvium of a carp
waited,
between banks, for you

to seize it

and, in a river
of elided letters
of drowned predicates
there drifted
something like your name,
a solitude spelt backwards
amid noctambulant voices

trailing a face
a boss, scored featureless
by wind and rain,
heat and cold,
and time

but you would never
pronounce it.

A Boyhood

Not a sound
through the dark
air only
a dog barking
click of a dynamo
on spokes, before sleeping

house fronts.
Cold latches.
Environs, barred
to him. Days
held in the element
of despair, floated

up a hill
past the wooded
moat of sky. To
where, and who,
beyond himself,
was watching, if at all

the land forming
round a question,
river moving
through its treacherous sediments,

Shoreditch, Purfleet, Gravesend,
while the marsh burned

white flesh from stalks
and the church threw
its pointed shadow across
the vigour of
a dead pastoral. Ominous
succession of signs; words

to denigrate
the shape of the tongue, stuttering
father's employment, school.
Supineness before authority.
'The best infantry in the world.'
He heard

the afternoon sigh
on the ragged verges
of council estates,
where the shop fronts creaked
out of their
broken names and hoardings

'Alston, Edwards, Nunn,'
generations that stayed,
and the light, pouring
through orchards and graveyards,
and birdsong.
Journeys, beginning

and ending,
a twilight
of narratives. Where
the river moved
amid the summer spores,
nettles and dockleaves

through small creaks,
trickled, he wrote
his name
upon the softened stump
of a rotting aspen
branch, and launched it.

Flume

Rippled

tongue adrift
on shadows,
       pulled through
a world impatient
to sound

ledger of worn gleanings,
rustling drawers,
the night's thin loams
   growing
whiter   towards dawn,
the names of the lost

particulars,
air, with all its
laminations
and distractions,

listening
to what breaks
across itself,
mirror colliding
with its reflection,
  syllable,
             calling

back what
the years discard,
      until you cannot hear
anymore
what it is they are

saying;
  cognate of
'to arrive,'
at a point
      — ad verbum —
where one is
always departing
                died

many times,
forehead pressed against
          wainscots
where you wrote
the names,
        and listened:
  they never
came back.

The freight
of 'here',
      lilacs
weaving

beyond shadows
             one white flake
upwards
     where

  are you
as the year ends,
under a token
of thunder,
then
        silence
reconfirming

  what is here
is at variance
  with itself

in the wind
    the slow
flowers of the talahib
    the kakawati

endlessly stream.

A Constructed Place

LIGHT WHERE THERE IS

A figment
the whole drift
and slew

of air
fricatives colliding
in an empty place

leaves surrender
careless effigies
of who we are

and   insistent
light where there is
dark undergrowth

grown daily
more rank
within   extremities

of pain   But —
the air unheard
nonchalance pervading

itself and us
caught in the bend
of a wrist

transcribed
topography of sound
giving back what

we never were
can be
The grey face

in a rain of weeks
life dissolving
marls and toxins

And   as if
acacias were bent
shadows from the brim

of some immense
caprice a voice
a silence   It is

more than we deserve
knowing ourselves
so sparely to enun

ciate   So clear
Tides of a factory
scum foul odour

of regret for
things done not
done Yet

there is
joy simply
in the holding of

words on a page
that do not deliver us
from what we are.

ARCHIPELAGO NIGHTS

Bone white sheen,
and she has slipped
quietly away
from you in sleep,
the phosphorescence
of a shallow lingers
wide, enveloping
arm, leg

                              an anthem
of doomed corals,
a submerged republic
that rides up onto
the waters of the night,
bring back voices
over the surf, into
this quiet

                              who
shuffling back, late
from that shore
of lost spirits,
wasted no time
in enfolding, street
by street, an entire
imago, the chaos
of your life, in her mind

                                        a skull
of forsaken memories,
emporia of dreams, where
remains of the displaced
and the exploited grip
the eyes' ebb, flight
towards another coast
that's unenveigled, transparent

                                    gauging
the precise angle
of the head and feet, the
body's disposition, waits
among the abaca and
the looms of shipwrecked
hands, and dances,
though the signs
are not propitious

                    speaks
out of the dried up
reservoirs, the slums
of bought-off voters, declining
to name the price
of silence, her hands
arranging the wreaths
of victims, spread
and undressed

                    binds,
with a calla lily,
the broken waist
of the water,
a bracelet of tiny scars
round her wrist,
the blood of indentured labourers
on haciendas
darkening her streams

                    drawn
into each small
hollow, cove, breathing
an exile's prayer, an anthem
of deception,
the filth of clogged esteros
filling the streets,
you wait,
uneasily, on the night's
escarpment of bone,

                    where
flotsam, gulls,
and driftwood meet
the horizon, level with the edge
of some glittering repose,
the heart pounds
solitary, moving
between itself and others,

                    clear
light of moon
to navigate you through
reefs, drawing
around you a fleet of ghosts,
words — *land reform,*
abolition of oligarchy —
tilling air
to see
what will grow
on shifting current.

                    Thin,
like a wafer,
they dissolve
upon the tongue . . .
indigent's breath,
crepuscular
flower of the retreating
jungle, invoking them
you invoke yourself,
again

amidst a catafalque
of blooms, of horns.
In desolate barrios,
bound for foreign
aquariums, the doomed
corals of the republic
raise, like bleached bone,
their branches up
into an air in which
they drown.

A Habitation

The snowdrops, broken necked on tall stems under the trees, have gone. Terracotta sun plaques line the sandstone walls of the courtyard. A curlew falls above a far off meadow. Where do the clouds go, but to the edge of the horizon. We are orphaned almost as soon as we can talk from the wind that leaves no names inside us. The river, a harried sound now over the earth's shoulder, echoes through the panes of the empty summerhouse and beside the drained swimming pool. Each day the sensations of our past come back to haunt us. Broken laughter at the top of steps, a particular look, smell, the angle of light across a face or sward of grass. They ripple on the desks at which we sit poring over our dictionaries, catalogues and compendiums, the conduits of a place which we construct. Beyond the sound of all the words is the sound of the air, breathing. An empty road on the brow of a hill defines the limits of our field of vision. Maybe, though, if we were to utter our names again in the wind it would come back without them – having gathered, from these worn out and debilitated siftings, the source of all the names; that deep vacancy and stillness towards which each day the mind, along with the tired echo from the empty summerhouse, bends. And from which the swimming pool drains a slow fosse of light which ripples at the edge, as if it was filling.

THE BLESSING

Tamarinds ripen above the dust of a bare compound.
We look at one another, and do not know if what we see
is compliant with our looking, or looking away.
I put down two peso coins on a counter.
Tomorrow they could be worthless as dirt.
Sunlight on the terracotta steps. On the flag
stones of the courtyard snow melts
around a hardening absence. No lexicon can arrange
each nuance of everything that has happened.
We open our eyes much later, and sift
what there is left. Too much has gone, or was
not there in the first place. So where, and how
did the argument begin? Where does the road run,
across an open plain, or under trees? All day, all night
an offshore breeze blows over the mangroves.
Your breath was like the very faint odour of a flower.
Everything bends and buckles. Nothing is,
continually, what it appears to be. Even the past
has been manipulated, Abueva's sculpted figures
from concocted dynasties glistening at the edge
of a decaying campus. What does the wind know,
ravelling itself into our homes, navigating
the slim estuaries of our locks? How solitary
the roads are that we set out on, even though we
do not wander down them alone. Across the river,
above the tilth of a dark ridge, an owl hunts
under a full moon. Your hand was like a small square, a sky
into which someone had hurled a blessing, and then gone home.

This Tutelary Space

In this idealised space, if you listen carefully as you turn from one street into another, you hear your breath and, in an ancient topography of sound, passing the citadels and shrines of all the various tutelary spirits who have at one time or another inhabited and been worshipped in the squares and places your passing shadow brushes against, you sense not only the dark of your own respiration but the 'gates' through which the fluxion of so many prayers of previous generations of pilgrims and exiles before you have entered. Indeed, you begin to feel, walking up and down these streets, that your own physiology is the site of a continuous liturgy, a repetition whose rhythm, if you could only manage to succeed in falling into step with it, would end, ultimately, in the act of your own disappearance. Repeating the syllables which seem vicariously to come into your mind you begin to lose sense of any distinct direction in which you might be headed, and in your increasingly insistent circumambulations, over a ground which appears to be homologised with a transcendent plane, you sense, if nothing else, the regressive structure of your movement, syllable and word drifting on a current of air where the ghosts of sounds, like carbonised outlines on the steps of some irradiated city, are indelibly impressed. Each street which you walk up and then down comes to seem the same, whichever end you approach it from. Likewise the letters of their names, when repeated, eventually, robbed of the authority of their power of designation, seem not to suggest difference so much as the mere interstices of your breath, holding within themselves a variance which is at the same time in agreement with itself—reversed, they would make just as much 'sense'. What are these words, then, you think, and the objects which they denote, but portals through which, if you could pass freely from the chaos and longing of your own life, would open onto nothing except an empty space. A space in which there would be nothing to pronounce. Only, within the memory of that self you could not deliver yourself from, and in the darkness of light and in the endless sacrifice of night to morning, a long strained for, and sought after, erasure

RESIDUES OF LIGHT AND AIR

The Pear Tree

Irresolute border. The wind shifting in
the hedgerow. Immaculate white lawn of
snow. Pale light moving across the river.

Where a face turned behind a curtain,
refulgent in shadow. Was it the curve of
the mind—the breath's camber—or a real figure.

For daylight's first loss, recorded nothing
but this. Beyond an open window night,
an immeasurable sadness of streets,
filling the intervals of a life.

Glow on buildings, railroads clanking in
the dawn's stillness, the smell of livestock.

And nothing differs, except the difference
of loss and gain. A memory of distinct
horizons and spaces, peopled by a question.

Rockpools. Calendulas in churches.
Tracing a likeness out of despair.

The pear tree filtering — like a great web of
suspended motes — air: looking up into it.

Would solve nothing, landscape, dream
figure that a mind makes, shifting
between itself and that imagined other.

Desire reduced to a brisk metaphor of exchange,
consumed, burned by its own transport.
Damp bodies, gathering sand on the world's littoral.

What we proceed towards through the
night's humidity day's rancour, tinkle

of goat bells across a far river bloom
of white dust upon dead words.

My darkling syllable strung upon a high
cloister, echo I listen for, faded angelus,
fingertap upon my broken window.

Turns, turns the light on in each dark
corner. "In the softly luminous hour tell
me a story, where nothing is more than
itself, an object turning in its own memory."

Is only this: an ember of dusk, caught in
the wind; a shadow that calls to us out of
an aperture in a garden wall, from another country.

THAMES

grey chaffing at the lane's end when you went by a stone in
the palm of your hand

rolling it backwards and forwards as if it was a name you
could not quite pronounce a

body here where the mind cannot divide it of water
without a geography one moment

caught up by the next bereft moving towards what's gone
what's to come table lamp

beside a bed a book open at a page that must have meant
something once made it run

beneath those sour fogs smelling of gas under broken lamp
posts un–uttering yourself

making a voice a replica of it through your hands between
two exiles into the faded

nomenclature of its reaches that were drought ridden frozen
and fever warped acres of

your own body under the lamp where you breathed
acanthus drowned in its peremptory

calling word sound that moved wind battered slewed over
your tongue to dissolve

now in all of its fold ings and cold ripples upon no

                                                    thing

EDGES

Body that has no country
no map, no horizon to navigate by.
It sets out on,
and is the sole author of,
its own journey.
Unannounced, always
unexpectedly taking off
into the blue of elsewhere;
bowsprit, the ideal music
of the purest memories
that have been ground down
into disconsolate atmospheres
in which we are waiting, breathing
the air of some where else.

In the reinstated constituents
of time and space, standing
outside a bookstore, the *Solidaridad*
on Padre Faura, thinking
what is the light doing
looking for a place
in which it could belong, watching
the dust turn ceaselessly
under the acacia trees.

Impermanent blue
shadow,
the treacherous edge
of a 'here'.
The wisp of a wind
would blow it away,
into a sky woven with
promises. It follows us
with the shape of leaking horizons,
the grey impersonations of waves
          that break upon
rooms filled with the saddest
of roses, of old photographs,
a haunting chemistry that blows
from some remote topography:
                    sounds
through an open window
that no one has heard before
or composed.

Place of unconnected moments
of infinite arrivals and farewells,
of a sail on a shore.
Whose is this face that we seem to remember
but can't quite recall:
the discarded fragment of a dream,

perhaps, a melody, intended to lead us
back to where it began.
Half heard conversations.
Unrecuperable names.
They shelve away down
to a broad sunlit avenue,
to trees that ripple
on a white plain
where lightning lacerates a dark sky.

In the stillness of 'not moving'
someone,
suddenly, thinks *home.*
Dark petals
on a sill, a lace
curtain bending in,
corroborate, and mock,
    a sense of being
somewhere else.

Ideal place of memories:
                    glimpsed —
            then gone.

Lisping,
sometimes, in the coordinates
of a lost tongue
it brings back to us
                    nothing
but the kapoc tree at night in bloom
and the shadow of the one
who passed under it,
at noon, muttering
who am I, carving
his signature out of the wind.

BELONGING

To no where
to no thing
to the shortest abridgement
   of air   of word
to   the cruel insignia
         of our acquisitions.

Lost
under damp swamp of cloud
    muddy field
        the moon
's light
     very first embrace.
  Still missing.

The scent of what lies
 at the end of the road;
    a copse
of guava trees, perhaps,
    or tamarind:
  suffused in the wind,
gathering   and dispersing.

Flame
in windless rain
that keeps   burning
hand
of the one who doubts.
The sound
of a pure line of thought   running
carrying over
into the present.
Beside the table   a blue chair
with all the confidence of
a disclosure
leaning into space
and silence.

To no particular
time   or place
then.
Under the shadow   of the rain trees
I saw her hurrying
towards what
was only
a distant speckle of light
upon a   possible event.

                    Heard
        in the rustle of
that air,   as it was
                          departing,
    another moment   arising.
              A history
of burned pages.

Cannot come back
        cannot, ever,
                        return to
        where it was,
                        crushed between
those pale linens
                        a sprig
    of purple   sweetening
            the tongue.

Was
the width of a breath
 between us,   crossing
the hot courtyard,
              unable to compose
ourselves   through all those
       annihilations
we had not spoken of
   over which we
 had no control.

The dark saxifrages,
  in a crevice
on a slope,   bending
   in the breeze
of a bright morning
              having,
      unlike ourselves,
                   no need
   to locate
just where they are.

Move
          across
this sandstone wall
          this acropolis of air
your voice
               so that the emptiness may spall
                         and stain
          into it.

          For
     what we are
                    excluded from,
          the roots' white
                    intricate knot,
                         air
through the thin shadows of our bodies
               refutes,
          grinding the rocks
under our feet   dissolving
          the black ashes of words
               in our throats.

Signifies only
    what it does not
        possess
but will go on   looking
    for
among all the vagaries and evaporites
    that attend it
           leaving
in this trackless dust
    a footprint,
    the pale ghost
of a voice
        crossing a road.

The *English* Boat

"I see that the birds are flown".
King Charles I

"We are
Those Fractions of the Sum of Being, far
Dis-spent and foul disfigured, that once more
Strike for Admission at the Treasury Door".

Farrid ud-Din Attar

LIQUID GOLD

In England under a grey suborned light many years ago, in air
etched with bickering, birdsong—*Turdus merula*: ornate variant
of a rotundity expiring, through arboreal gloom, in a scratchy
finale. Suddenly. Like an indecipherable signature, annotating a
tract in which we had all conspired. Whose ink the centuries
have dilated into this note. Lilac scent heavily drifting in from
a garden. The past, in which we were all remembered without
being named / performing all the obeisances and making 'the
right noises', warbled. A scribbled note to those who might pass
that way through the wood again. A little gold in the margin.
Sifted song.

Farewell to the Shade

These twits and twoos, on a night of frost and bare trees. Sonority that will breathe in the deciduous wood, when the wood is no more. Thaumaturgic, rising when the King is no more, as the moon rises above the hedgerow, laden with pageantry and no words — the great landed estates, the gentry and the freeholders, gone / 6000 mature oaks for a man-o-war / for a parliament to grant a king his pocket money. "To whit To who" — to that which exists, *Strix aluco*, in the mind only, apropos the heart, what we have wrested from arboreal carnage. Between closely pressed palms the sound of a nation transcendent, its geist. Even a tree can be without existing.

Kaah-kaah-kaah

On churchyard oak and immemorial elm, *Corvus frugilegus*, a parliament of dark chattering. Under a pall of smoke Drogheda burns. A man winces in pain, implores mercy. Bludgeoned with his wooden prosthetic limb, he gets none. Thick roosting of shadows. Clusters of hawthorn blossom lining the August lanes shake in a thunderous roil of air. The carrion mouth of the moment opens upon "barbarous wretches" and their "corrupt customs . . . licentious swearers, and blasphemers, ravishers of women and murtherers of children". *Res nullius*. For a form of government and polity that brought "England . . . to the height of perfection and happiness". For a land "adorned with goodly woods even fit for building . . . ships . . . as if that some Princes in the world had them they would soon hope to be lords of all the seas". A "lande so fertile as wanteth nothinge"—four fifths of it manhandled from its rightful owners. High in their cold colony, *Corvus frugilegus,* pitched into the wind, descend above the outstretched shadow of a man.

'To Get the Pearl and Gold'

Over salty shallows the scent of jasmine and tobacco flower drifted. In unworked mines. In deep woods of oak "farre greater and better than in England" revenue for settlement. Timber for ships for a country almost depleted of it. El Dorado. Subtropical air. Wading warm waters. Oyster shell middens on the shore. Shad, sturgeon and turtle. Bear and elk. Sumpweed and marsh elder. Gourds, beans and squash. "Let cannons roar . . . Go, and subdue". A continent for their taking. All, one day, the disaffected of Europe. Destiny made manifest. Tearing "a . . . kinde and loving people . . . void of all guile and treason". 'Tearing' they came < from the Latin *vulturus*. To 'purify', as they might have said, the savagery of their heathenish ways and days < from the generic *Cathartes*. So as the sun went down above the hills of Roanoke Island, *Cathartes aura*, nostrils perforate and lacking a syrinx, grunted and hissed from a dead tree defecating on its legs to dissipate heat. Was that not a voice which was prophetic of what was to succeed it—appetency and fear? Grunted, and hissed. Contrasted, or not really, with that sweetly anointed tongue: "only my father would keep such a bird in a cage"? Journeying from Munster estates of forfeited land across the sea to her—"the Ladie of the sea". Composing an encomium. Accompanied by another who sang, also, sweetly to her. His song, upon that "interminable waterway" that reached to the farthest ends of the earth, running softly in his companion's ear.

OUT IN THE OPEN

Among the whitethorn hedges, beds of burdock and nettle. On the lichened tree trunks light, a golden wash. Scent of hellebore and vetch. Small ploughed fields fenced in where once there would run to the horizon common and meadow pasture, manorial wastes, marsh. Song of *Carduelis chloris, Turdus viscivorus* usurping that of *Vanellus vanellus, Numencus minutus, Perdix perdix*. From exiled song retain, on the wind, crunch of grubbed up livelihood of centuries fed to the sheep's gut, silence of grass growing in doorways and floors of abandoned houses, felling of wood and copse. And sound of a gentry chewing, growing fat on its appropriations of land increasing rapidly in value fifty fold. Cottagers and commoners deprived of acreage for grazing their cattle, sheep and geese, for berrying, gleaning, fetching fuel, hunting and cultivating; turned into paupers or, no longer independent, fodder for factories in cities. And, if they stubbornly resisted, hung, disembowelled and dismembered. From a parliament of landlords plush on its hassocks and rents, retain, too, the refrain "to labour every day in the year" their children "put out to labour early" so that the "subordination of the lower ranks of society . . . would thereby be considerably secured". And then turn, again, to this neat arcadia of cottages and small fenced in fields with their hedgerows a foam of blossom—over them the ethereal anodynes of a popular imagination hover, the hoarse perorations of politicians held hostage by sybaritic noise, the importunings of investors, the unending inanities of celebrities and their besotted and gloom-laden inquisitorial media—and inhale, deeply, the old lie of a bucolic idyll.

Siempre Leal Ciudad

On the black sands of Malate, "O brave new world", Tar and Sepoy. Biting the briny biscuit—tea from China—keels hauled up beneath nipa village. Over foothills and foreshore *Penelopides manillae,* its nasal 'eenk', cheap toy trumpet, floated by them over the water. To be supplemented much later, under a steady drizzle, by that Yankee ("Aves de Repina") 'There'll be a Hot Time in the Old Town Tonight'. Floating, up the Camino Real, over—here, take this proffered hand of duplicity—a breastwork of bodies, to alight on the ear of, saunterers on the Escolta/ practitioners of diverse dialects and languages, "naked savages". Bone peg through nose, dyed terracotta molars, sitting astride a flush toilet. "Cultivated and educated" at last. O, "Ye gentle birdes, the worlds faire ornament/And heavens glorie", look at us now.

A PLACE INSUFFICIENTLY IMAGINED

The astonished white wave broke and ran amidst red-fruited ketaki thickets; amidst "streets large and well paved, the Trade great . . . the Merchants rich, the Artificers excellent"; amidst "gardens planted with fruitfull Trees and delightful Flowers . . . [where] they have pleasant Fountaynes to bathe in, and other delights by sundrie conveyances of water, whose silent murmure helps to lay their senses with the bonds of sleepe in the hot seasons of the day". And stopped. *That alone being Real which is in itself, which does not need anything to be what it is.* "Their chiefe idoles bee blacke and evill-favoured, their mouthes monstrous". As observed by their "stupid idolatries" they "ground their opinions upon tradition, not Reason". So, eventually, the age old right to collect land revenues was extended to foreigners—a new and "violent" regime of collection. The master weaver craftsmen of Dhaka stood with bleeding hands, index fingers and thumbs severed, a generation of teachers— never such fine muslin lace, 1,800 threads to the inch, again woven—obliterated, all for a refusal to grow indigo. And so the land, grain reserves having been prohibited and many fields once sown with grain forcibly given over to indigo and cotton bound for overseas markets, exhausted, yielded famine. A third of the population dead. And profit. "There had been nothing like it since the Spanish Conquistadores looted the Aztec and Inca civilizations". And opium, spices and precious stones. "Enormous profit" stoked the furnaces of a Revolution, its "structural development" at "every possible level", back home. Ash-grey, deceiving bird, *Cuculus varius*, 'pipieeta . . . pipieeta' endlessly amidst the kitaki trees, using an other's nest, lining its own.

Through starching heat, through blood red leaves of the fire trees and silent fierce white compounds at noon, comes, up the long shaded corridor of the close, that note again.

Customs / Duties

At the customs house at the Ch'ung-wen Gate the grasses are
high as a man's waist. Over the October river the plaintive 't-e-
e-e' of *Chaimarrorius leucocephalus*. The Bogue forts are black
with fire and smoke. For a couple of razed and looted palaces,
for a nation forced to consume the cakes of a debilitating
and fatal bliss, for an unequal treaty and five million ounces
of silver (recriminatory indemnity) > two knighthoods. For a
horde of hovering missionaries and merchants, for a yawning
trade deficit > a deep and an abiding, "undermining our good
customs and morality", resentment. The Bogue forts black with
fire with smoke. For ten thousand released chests of seized
contraband and "a barren rock". For an ignored testimonial,
"Your Majesty has not before been thus officially notified . . .
that we mean to cut this harmful drug" > the "matter *in sich*"
is deferred. In the snow's fallen silence "a hundred years of the
saddest news"—we had fed the heart on "translucencies". "A
road for none but the birds".

"THEY CANNOT BE TAUGHT LESSONS"

Over the harbour mouth shadow of *Milvus migrans* buoyant upon thermals, scavenging air, migratory amidst the fractured plumage of a world of opportunity and loss, surveying estuary and coastline. Lisped in corridors and classrooms of immense light, the sounds of a strange language. Form, without conviction, of objects (horse chestnut tree) never before seen. Sound divested of sense. Disadvantaged from the start. All subjects rendered through a fatiguing alpha, beta—shrivelling the calligrapher's art (and heart). A "red plague rid you/For learning me your language". A half understood semaphore brandished in the dark, retarding intellectual/emotional development. A parody, at best, of over enunciated moaning, of an over-wrought Tennysonian eclogue of sound. Rewarded with prizes from speaking competition judges, places at university, a well paid job.

Heart of Oak

Unable to transcend, theodolite in hand draining swamp drawing a map laying down a road, that *idée fixe* > the continuity of the moment's succession. Unassailable identity, sustained—exalter of Time, its self-styled acme and amanuenses—through an imagined catenation. Driven from a cramped fog infested island of stewed cabbage and curses by the trade winds, by a warm air of deliverance from all that tethered, restrained. Greeted by the fluty song, 'we-weeleow', of *Oriolus chinensis* over the bamboo thickets again and again. But to have listened, in that song, to what, again, was only a *similar* succession of events, or notes. And, further, not to have discerned that the silence in the silence which followed it was not the real silence but, furled in each other, silence&song, the dissolution of all silence and all sound > was to have missed an opportunity unequalled. So, many years later, holds full of bullion, they would return. Return to a song (one which re-cognised would always sound the same), but no silence. A silence, but no song. To an empty wood with an idol placed within it. Reared with the profits from a world it sacked. Bloated by half-blinding kudos. Fed on blood of wars. Gouging the earth it stood on. Its devotees a horde of hungry wasps drowning in syrups. Its priests a long line of profane white garbed technicians pandering to its wants.

"Why all those birds?"

Mapping from the coastline all the way to the interior. By the Darling River, between the pineapple plantation and the orchards, a navigation light. Legend of footpaths > gentle/ steep or seasonally overgrown/indistinct or obscure. Gradient, height, contour. Mapping, as adjunct, no inner space. No ordinance of emotion, cognition. Cartography of phantasms, ghosts. Each periplus a palimpsest. Each Crow. Each Eaglehawk. A superstition. Rather than complementary markers in an interfluous circuit. Imitating. Embroidering. Singing the other's song. The first notes, varied, recombining into the last. The last repeated, in another guise. So that the harmony might reassert itself. A circuit. So that what *is*, Eaglehawk / Crow, might imagine itself as, transform itself into, what it *is not*. The sound of its imagined other, that which is not-in-itself, floating by it on the river and through the trees.

DIOMEDEA EXULANS

Out of frozen wastes of sea. Precipices of water. Ten years
without sight of land. *Diomedea exulans*, held in the wind, sliding
and pulled by the current, higher and lower. Until both the
descent and the ascent seem to coincide in its 'motionless' body,
which seems neither to move away from nor toward us. Whose
motion, *though its beginning must be seen to occur as a thing in the*
present motion is only detectable at a point in the past or the future,
begins nowhere. 'Waa-waa-waa'. Fragment of a call, faltering
in these "forever exiled waters". In dark sleet. In driving cloud.
Vocable born beyond the rim of the Great World. A language
we do not own or possess. Owning the oceans. Annexing the
lands beneath them. Littering the seaways—where suddenly
all the birds have fallen silent, the fish left. Ghosts calling
from the withered land of surplus value, from a dark dream
that consumes them: 'Save us'. Write on these planks with the
ocean's pen—in that same voice that long ago he sent back
across the sea to her—the names of each product. Pipes; stems
fashioned from the long hollow bones of its wings. Tobacco
pouches; stitched from the large webs of its feet. Slippers; sewn
from its soft downy white skin.

HOME

Unshrieved by song. The familiar coast welcomed them. Not
birds but men. So in love with Time, with all its divisions and
subdivisions, and with the synchronisation of the successive
moment. Beat in their blood and their head. Under the scars
of an ancient compulsion, the amputee stirred. Sound of *Turdus
merula*. Flight of that note through the deep wood again. Outside
of time. Not man but bird. Not bird but man. Neither different.
Nor identical. And wove, through the fractured circuit of the
bone and skin, a hand again. Not just a hand but, out of that
"elementary logic", a wing.

The ink has turned to dust. In the margin a scribbled portrait of a
bird, singing. Beyond it, in that garden still from which, like
Wang Chih from Stone Bridge Mountain, he had returned
after what he thought was only a moment but which was
a hundred years, its note.

Notes

Title Page
Andrew Marvell, *Bermudas.*

Farewell to the Shade
Title: William Cowper, *The Poplar-Field.*
Line 7–8: William Shakespeare, *Love's Labour's Lost.*

Kaah–Kaah–Kaah
Line 7: Oliver Cromwell; after the taking of Drogheda.
Line 7–9: Edmund Spenser, *A View of the State of Ireland.*
Line 9: *res nullius*—Roman law by which all unoccupied
    or under-utilized lands remained common property of
    mankind. Primary argument used in planting Munster and
    Ards. Iterated in John Locke's *The Second Treatise of Civil
    Government.*
Line 10–11: Richard Hadsor, *Discourse on the Irish State.*
Line 11–14: Edmund Spenser, *op.cit.*
Line 14: Sir William Herbert, *Croftus Sive de Hibernia Liber.*

To Get the Pearl and Gold
Title: Michael Drayton, *To the Virginia Voyage.*
Line 2–3: Arthur Barlowe, *The Roanoke Voyages 1584–1590.
    Documents to Illustrate the English Voyages to North America
    Under the Patent Granted to Walter Raleigh in 1584.*
Line 7–8: Michael Drayton, *op.cit.*
Line 9–10: Arthur Barlowe, *op.cit.*
Line 9–11: T.S. Eliot, *The Waste Land.*
Line 19–20: Prince Henry eldest son of James 1st (Referring
    to Sir Walter Raleigh).
Line 21: Edmund Spenser, *Colin Clout.* (Referring to
    Elizabeth 1st and to Raleigh's poem *[The Ocean to] Scinthia*
    addressed to the Queen, but never circulated).
Line23: Joseph Conrad, *Heart of Darkness.*

Out in the Open
Line 18–21: Board of Agriculture Report quoted by
    Christopher Hill in *Reformation to Industrial Revolution.*

Siempre Leal Ciudad
Title: King Phillip II of Spain.
Line 1: William Shakespeare, *The Tempest.*
Line 6: Nick Joquin, *Manila my Manila.*
Line 10–12: Dean C. Worcester—US Secretary of Interior for
    the Philippines (1914).
Line 12–13: Edmund Spenser, *Prothalamion.*

A Place Insufficiently Imagined
Line 2–3: Edward Terry, as quoted in Samuel Purchas,
    '*Hakluytus Postumus or Purchas His Pilgrimes*'.
Line: 4–8: William Finch, as quoted in Samuel Purchas, *op.cit.*
Line 10–12: William Finch, as quoted in Samuel Purchas, *op.cit.*
Line 14: attributed to Governor-General Warren Hastings.
    "Seven entire battalions were added to our military
    establishment to enforce the collections . . . [that] carried
    terror and ruin through the country"— Robert Orme,
    official historiographer of the East India Company. Orme
    resigned in protest in 1762.
Line 22–24: Christopher Hill, *Reformation to Industrial
    Revolution.*
Line 25–26: Nicholas Dirks, *The Scandal of Empire.*

Customs / Duties
Line 9–10: Chinese Government Proclamation (1810).
Line 13–14: Commissioner Lin Zexu, letter (1839) to Queen
    Victoria.
Line 12: Lord Palmerston.
Line 14: T.S. Eliot, Introduction to *Selected Poems, Ezra Pound.*
Line 15–16: Tu Fu, *Autumn Meditation.*
Line 16: T.S. Eliot, *op.cit.*
Line 16–17: Tu Fu, *op.cit.*

They Cannot Be Taught Lessons

Title: Peter Martyr of Anghiera, *De Orbe Novo.*
Line 9–10: William Shakespeare, *The Tempest.*

Why All Those Birds?

Title: Radcliffe-Brown quoted by Claude Lévi-Strauss in
    Totemism.

Diomedea Exulans

Line 9: Herman Melville, *Moby-Dick.*

Home

Line 10: Claude Lévi-Strauss, *Totemism.*

The Ink Has Turned to Dust . . .

Title: A Spanish legend, according to which—as recounted by
    Robert Louis Stevenson—a monk who had been distracted
    from his copy-work by the song of a bird went out into the
    garden to listen more closely. When he returned, after what
    he thought were only a few minutes, he discovered that a
    century had gone by, that his fellow monks were dead and
    his ink had turned to dust.
Line 3: Meng Chiao, *The Stones where the Haft Rotted.* The
    poem's epigraph reads: "Wang Chih of the Chin dynasty
    (265–419) went into the mountains to gather firewood and
    saw two boys playing chess. The boys gave him a thing like
    a date stone, which he ate, and satisfied his hunger. At the
    end of the game, the boys pointed and said. "Look! Your
    axe handle is rotten." When Chih returned to his village, he
    was a hundred years old". Meng Chiao's poem begins: "Less
    than a day in paradise".